Made in United States
Orlando, FL
28 November 2023

39677628R00061